Do I want to trav(
marry...

What brings me joy in life...

I want to change the world by.....

My dream career is....

Is it my goal to relocate to a new area after my education...

The first thing I will do on vacation is.....

The world will change a lot in the next five years....

_____

_____

_____

_____

_____

_____

_____

_____

_____

_____

_____

_____

_____

_____

_____

_____

_____

_____

What type of area will I live in as an adult city or country...

My dream vacation is....

My best friend is fun because....

I am motivated by...

What do you think the world will be like in 2313?

_____

_____

_____

_____

_____

_____

_____

_____

_____

_____

_____

_____

_____

_____

_____

_____

_____

If you could travel anywhere with a time machine, where would you go?

If you had the chance to see what your life would be like in 20 years, would you take it?

The season I am happiest in is.....

I make my best decisions when...

_____

_____

_____

_____

_____

_____

_____

_____

_____

_____

_____

_____

_____

_____

_____

_____

_____

The one place I must visit is....

Is dating a good idea now...

My dream summer job is...

My life plan includes...

If I could change my name it would be.....

I want to go to college in the city /
country because .....

_____

_____

_____

_____

_____

_____

_____

_____

_____

_____

_____

_____

_____

_____

_____

_____

_____

How can I prevent peer pressure from causing me to make mistakes...

The reason I am special is.......

_____

_____

_____

_____

_____

_____

_____

_____

_____

_____

_____

_____

_____

_____

_____

_____

_____

I like to play a musical instrument because....

How will the Internet change in the next 30 years?

_____

_____

_____

_____

_____

_____

_____

_____

_____

_____

_____

_____

_____

_____

How will I fund college...

Where do you see yourself in 15 years?

_____

_____

_____

_____

_____

_____

_____

_____

_____

_____

_____

_____

_____

_____

_____

_____

My dream day to myself is....

_____

_____

_____

_____

_____

_____

_____

_____

_____

_____

_____

_____

_____

_____

_____

_____

_____

_____

_____

_____

Is volunteer work important...

_____
_____
_____
_____
_____
_____
_____
_____
_____
_____
_____
_____
_____
_____
_____
_____
_____

My funniest moment was....

The best book I have read is......

_____

_____

_____

_____

_____

_____

_____

_____

_____

_____

_____

_____

_____

_____

_____

_____

_____

What will people of the future think of our world when they look back to today?

_____

_____

_____

_____

_____

_____

_____

_____

_____

_____

_____

_____

_____

_____

_____

_____

_____

Five goals for my life after high school.....

_____

_____

_____

_____

_____

_____

_____

_____

_____

_____

_____

_____

_____

_____

_____

_____

_____

Do my dreams include having a family?

I like to play sports because....

_____

_____

_____

_____

_____

_____

_____

_____

_____

_____

_____

_____

_____

_____

_____

_____

Who am I...what do I want in life...

How will your life change as you get older?

I like to write because....

By the time you're an adult, what new
advances in technology do you think you
will see?

What will computers of the future look like?

My dream G.P.A. is.....

Will I care more about money or creativity in life?

Five goals for the college years...

Will the career I want to pursue support the type of life I want to have...

The best day in my life was.....

My dream spouse is....

An adventure I would like to have is....

18632075R00031

Made in the USA
Middletown, DE
30 November 2018